CW00927097

Hauntings at the Hour of Noon

Hauntings at the Hour of Noon

Poetry & Prose

rebeccca leanne claire gimblett

gatekeeper press™

Tampa, Florida

This book is a work of fiction. The names, characters and events in this book are the products of the author's imagination or are used fictitiously. Any similarity to real persons living or dead is coincidental and not intended by the author.

The views and opinions expressed in this book are solely those of the author and do not reflect the views or opinions of Gatekeeper Press. Gatekeeper Press is not to be held responsible for and expressly disclaims responsibility for the content herein.

Hauntings at the Hour of Noon: Poetry & Prose

Published by Gatekeeper Press
7853 Gunn Hwy, Suite 209
Tampa, FL 33626
www.GatekeeperPress.com

Copyright © 2023 by rebeccca leanne claire gimblett
All rights reserved. Neither this book, nor any parts within it may be sold or reproduced in any form or by any electronic or mechanical means, including information storage and retrieval systems, without permission in writing from the author. The only exception is by a reviewer, who may quote short excerpts in a review.

The editorial work for this book is entirely the product of the author. Gatekeeper Press did not participate in and is not responsible for any aspect of this elements.

Library of Congress Control Number: 2023937831

ISBN (paperback): 9781662940118
eISBN: 9781662940125

*Those ghosts who went
North, South, East, and West
and those that came back*

Forward

A letter regarding the author, *rebecca leanne claire gimblett*:

In the process of curating my new self and lamenting the past self that this book encompasses; I felt all things from start to finish and then from the start again. Old lives not yet forgotten, or unable and unwilling to be forgotten, are making themselves known to me. This white oak family reunion.

Those past versions in me prove themselves not dead but are also not immortalized, like her, the character of me in this book, is. But they deserve honorarium, they are equally important in our journey together. And so, I come to you from the future to weave them into the fabric of this story too.

I was *rebecca leanne* first; small and shy with a propensity for odd behaviours like stuffing teddy bear fluff up my nose, and marking a spot in my room as the pee corner for reasons I cannot understand beyond laziness and then habit.

I was *rebecca leanne claire* next; an act of bipartisanship at age 11, already placating both sides instead of choosing myself. All the mediation, the secrets shared with me, my own mostly kept, and the many battles in the all-girls catholic primary school, st. josephs, where I was reared.

I was *bec, becca, bex* then. Learning about humans and the prison-style relationships you build in secondary school. Learning to drink, to kiss if you're lucky, finding love, breaking my heart, reaching beyond myself, and settling back again, often for less. Here I was alive as long as possible, trying on different skins and separating from them again.

Since 21, I have had a thousand names, all of them *Gimblett*. This was the real era of this book – the death and rebirth and death and rebirth that happens in your 20's when you have a mother like I did. When you have any trouble at all, really.

It sometimes feels like lying, all this part of me I kept hidden, waiting for the proper excavation. It also feels like vanity, pretending that all the wonderful people around me didn't see through every inch of me and loved me for each part I was struggling with. Please know that if you knew me at all in my life, you still know me now - here is just more of me. I want you to have all of me. I want you to see the corners you once knew and sand them soft. I want you to open the windows and clear out the cobwebs that are keeping visitors blind. To add the right spectrum of light needed to disempower secrets.

This book is an act of apocalypse, of revolution, of magic. Because living is an act. Of apocalypse. Of revolution. Of magic.

There are many to thank for it, to thank for me now, talking to you from the future present, to thank for helping me forwards, for giving me a chance.

Specifically.

Darcie: You were my everything and will always be. I would have died without you.

Tori, you are my bright hope, my mirror, I am your mirror, this reflective bond is infinite and unbreakable. I would have died without you.

Elaine, Killian, Aoife – you brought bex to life and gave her a proper chance at happiness. I might have died without you.

Mairead, Aisling, Marianne – you held me and taught me the power of stability and good love; I might have died without you.

Ruth, you almost killed me, and you were a portal to weirdness and learning and laughter and magic. I forgive you for my own broken heart.

Kate, we almost ran away together at age 10 – where would we be now?

Sarah – how young we were, thanks for being my first best friend.

Too many others, so many names kept in my heart, in the heart of this self and all my selves and all my namesakes alive, and the many many more friends and loves that are beside me right now, shepherding the future in, potentially unaware that they are carving out their roles in the next book.

But this one is for you and me.

Let me keep you alive and searching, let me join you for a moment on your circle, let time mean something to us.

I love you, in this life and many others, for the rest of time and whatever comes next,

beau

final note

This is a work of fiction in that it is an exploration of the mind, dreams, experiences, memories, thoughts and their breakdowns, feelings and their failures, possibilities, and history as posed by the author. They kept the words as true to the mission of honesty but with an emphasis on the exploration of alternate realities and alternate possibilities. If you think that you are in this book, it is not really you, it is a tiny molecule from space and time that the author pulled from thin air and molded from a memory - based entirely on perception and intuition - into something that fit a narrative need.

This is a work of fiction, a story shared by an often-unreliable narrator, built as an escape hatch as a means of survival.

It is the author's hope that you find your way to survive too.

Prelude

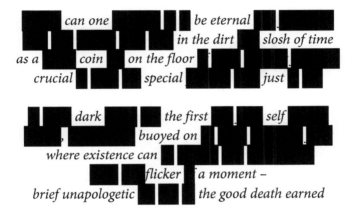

can one   be eternal
                 in the dirt   slosh of time
as a   coin   on the floor
crucial   special   just

        dark   the first   self
,   buoyed on
    where existence can
              flicker   a moment –
brief unapologetic   the good death earned

Contents

Part One

A Living: Existence with Struggle

What do you do when you've done everything?
- Do it again. Do better.

Integrity

Seek out loneliness
when you reach the limits
of solitude.
The limits are contentedness,
a satisfied full stomach. Seek
dissatisfaction: forget what you know
about trees. Don't seek
out people to fill the distance
between you and the void
you are edging towards.
Go further.
Further still,
find the room beneath the stairs
and read its sorrow walls.
Make cold your sceptre, wield it
on yourself. Be against others.
Loose the bungee cord grip
of what keeps you safe.
Safe is soft.
You can come back again, you know.
Soft is welcoming.
What animal is holding you back,
inviting you in? Burn it
in front of its mother's eyes,
her tears used
against rope-burn
on the way down.

Confessions in V parts

i

waste your days stuck in your own mind
in celebrated rules you break
in your heart the worst parts
are memory:
one, don't slap your sister's face
she doesn't deserve it
too young to know
you mimic. Two, always act loyally
believe in god and matrimony,
confess your sins, pray for forgiveness,
you'll need it. Three, love. respect
yourself. forgive yourself, can the rest
just choose a bit of these, or even one
and you'll be brave
and you'll be kind.
Oh my.
What have you done?

ii

waste your days living on trains
I thought you moved away
from home, the curling bite of sea
sells itself like Eastern merchants
out your pores. it salts the rain
and when you cry
it is only Poseidon
he misses you, love, he misses you
they all do, down there, in the tiniest
place in the world, the shops that paint
themselves new, the people who hate
why do they hate so many
useless things, where do they find the time?

you can't go back you'd wreck the place
you can't go back

come back, we miss you, darling
have you forgotten our motto is
though conquered we will not be subdued?
Nannie needs you to talk to, no one listens
to her stories, and Tori, it's a bad time
she only lights up when you send her
those messages online, are you really
that busy all the time?
and Joe, it's impossible to say
impossible, where will he go? He misses you
though he'll never admit it, of course, look
when he was reared. It's tough here at the mo,
we'll be here if you ever change your mind
but don't come home.

iii

waste your days upon the pen
online documents you type
why can't you get a real job?
why can't you ever sleep at night?
why can't you live on the breadline?
why can't you keep a social life?
why can't you eat more healthily?
why can't you keep that tongue
in that mouth? why can't you string
together a proper verse out loud?
where's your courage? where honest?
All I read is hidden things and no one
no one no one sees.
I told you to be patient.
I told you to be fine.
I told you to be balanced.
I told you to be kind.

iv

Let's take a break, admit out loud I'll make it.
I can take all the things in between the other things I do
and do not write. Like street urchins ache to survive, so do I.

v

Truth is that nothing is wasted
All is learning, all steam dries
Your character, clean and ready for the next
Truth is that I would not rather
Be gone, or dead, than running or fighting.
Truth is I fight for 50:50 chances sometimes.
Truth is I hate things: I hate guitar solos
They make me want to throw things
With impatience, like terrible action scenes. I hate small towns
They depress me, and crooked houses in city outskirts
Where you can't imagine anyone building anything new,
Ever leaving, ever living, holding hands soft.

Truth is I hated that last part of the journey
The 90 hours in a train to Canada from Yosemite.
I hated it, I knew I was losing myself, it was the
Beginning of that dirty business in LA, I want to say
I got nothing out of that journey. Truth is I'll never let it go.
Not the deer dancing at dawn in Utah? Truth is
Not old Irwin who bought us dinner in the carriage? Truth is
Not Chicago and the bead? Not the endless open mouth
Singing that America is. Truth is I hated it because
I lost you, the deadliest virus known to my species,
And still, still I blame myself for that. I always
Will.

rebecca leanne claire gimblett

all The wrong reasons

She asks why I go back Come back Be free
of this thing that keeps you grieving
How each lip you meet won't cure you
or absolve you like the lashing of a whip
could.
        She knows I find the worst things
appealing, but not why soaking
in sweet shallows How the pain
of love-blood does more for me
than healing water
would.
        I'm phobic, cold things. I stay up
close to fires, wrap in coveted layers of
old cloth and waxy drips and felt-off skin
as if stealing dirt from fabric could make up for it
- the other sin -
            Days pass
            but never a week
            between bells
            his bowerbird-echo
            my labrador-keening

each calculated thieving

The boy in all reflective glass passes me in the bus stop chalet
muttering, telling me this path will stop the madness like crying cants,
backwards on the ceiling
could.

Neck sinks, body sweeps
from side to side, snake
          -glance Next victim in an alleyway
first reapply make-up Last
          line of defence
by moonlight
          by rivershine

each emaciated gleaming

Back bent against nails scratch wood
Scrawl the beat of his sex inside me
laying groundwork Careless as lying

Come back Go back again When
my table top is not enough
I surrender in his kitchen

She asks me to remember this feeling.

Makes me describe it in great detail.

I will not know pity Naked again on the train
dig up the new grass from the well
she had me bury half-filled. Carry on
          one more push and the glass will fall out
          one last dull thump, he will peel and fall away
          once more

my insides
will
be contained.

rebecca leanne claire gimblett

living with it

By 5am, silent emotions are gas guzzled
down by night. Or rain sometimes
unheard until after.
Sky dancing to glimmer
magic that only works in shadow.

There's a pit in my heart I've been
digging at all day, for the night I get
to share some of this with someone
who has felt bare feet on a stairs

shadowed by skin and night dust, restless
as the world is asleep, not embarrassed
by life but ignited, knowing others not alone
are awake too, feeling something, anything.

heart

I let him make a circus of my life

He goes for sad men until they're sad for him, I mostly show them photographs where I smile and don't look at the camera, or

Laughing's better, attractive as a whale song or frog jump, as natural as the

True drunks are harmless, unable to hook or catch him; it's the moon he watches for

The return, to those I loved again and again, if at all possible, will be reused

Obsesses over two things, me and what is good, hoping with one, to find the other

Like two kids unable to stop from whispering while hiding

rebecca leanne claire gimblett

moonlighting

I have become the temporary love of this year's men when they see me

though phobic I am when people are watching

still they wish more of my future, less instability, lunacy

straighten me out with lists

1. *The dark line where the eye persists in seeing something that was never there to begin with.*

2. *a flat circle.*

by tides I turn things, towards and away

by saying Nothing is predetermined or foreseen

I am the one face they cannot make cry

I am the one

sinfully present, impatiently real

knowing Comfort

If the weather was with us, I'd have couches outside.
The garden would feel better for knowing comfort.

Great plush monsters of our parent's bad decisions
(what makes art but the next generation's rebelling)
red swirls of tough heartstring choices
the 70's were a fight to keep going.

I would know, look at my parents
- one likes the idea and one cannot get the idea right.

You are never what you are born into.

Couches in My Garden should have loved the air,
tensed at the scrawl peck and shit of birds
that make homes in anything they can at all.

rebecca leanne claire gimblett

seven Monday secrets

I am not afraid to buy cigarettes, I'm afraid to own them; I don't know how to not use things all up at once.

Friends are decent halfway houses, I store parts of my life I'm not fully ready for with them, they call me secretive but you aren't supposed to keep all your good jewels in one safe, the whole thing will run off one bad night.

I rotate in tentative circles towards change, make broad statements I believe in, no one else does. I have changed my life so many times, people are afraid to believe in their grip of me. I wear a jacket of loose hill grass from the side of a cliff.

She asked me how my life is different than how I thought it would be… I never thought many things beyond cool blue seas, propelling gear, the pinch of a harness.

That is how my life is different, safety gear.

My toolbox is full of jumble, I make it up as I go along.

going Back, moving Forward

Rebuilding,
he is hard in many wrong places,
running
hands over his silk cloth,
he
has cliffs.

I want to melt him.
I've been a drowner
since birth.
I could birth
little rocks for him, daughters
with unusual names,
happy minds. Sons made
from close hugging material.

He is wary of me, too much
and not enough -
I want and want, give and give
nothing asked.
Untouchable, I flap at him,
swing feral-like away
when his closed hands
hint

at 'seed',
or maybe 'beat'.

We balance
on a seesaw, four feet
off the ground, and YES of course YES

then I drop
then he drops

the angle of sight changes
sun filling up one
then the other
eye

giving all power to the feet
touching the ground

five woodsecrets

i

I wouldn't be telling just anyone this but I feel you would understand. There was a couch down there, it might have been leather but I think that was the other one, I believe this one was white, which would make sense, symbolic. White means more than leather, suggests less and this was a night of no suggestion, it was the backseat of a taxi to Wicklow, the speed of my tongue licking at the driver's past, asking, asking

ii

My jaw didn't like the forest, or maybe it misses the campfires, I still miss the smoke, smell it everywhere, probably just a bbq even though the year is still cold, probably car exhaust or cigarette tokes, but I can smell the wood, fresh from patient people's hands, saviours, heroes. Salutations, moon lovers

iii

I talked to three different trees specifically, all in general. I didn't need to dance, they were beautiful enough for us both, top tines twirling 360 then SUDDENLY their hips MIRACULOUSLY back again in the muted dawn, return return in tune with nothing.

Everything is green and grey, the smokescreen universe. Cheers went off like land was found: the generator failed, the generator went back on, wood was found, dancing began. I made wolves of us all. Jeff, Bronson, Biscuit Dancer, all howling, howling

iv

In the morning, people were replaced. A girl next to me on the couch.
She said "I hope I'm not pregnant". She said "I came to with my pants
around my ankles". I said "We'll raise this baby together." She said "I
don't know what I'll say to my boyfriend" I said "Don't tell him"… We
said. "Unless you need his support".
I didn't know where I stood on this. She knew which one.
I had just presumed we all had enough that no one would want more.

{I couldn't pull out the right emotion

and I thought maybe I didn't care and that scared me, I just wanted us

both to become stronger from this.

Bad things don't happen in the woods at night.

Too obvious.

There's a physical and chemical law stating

that "There was nothing I could have done" is a lie, only

inject yourself in and ask

"How did I come to this?"}

V

We left soon after and I put it, couch confessions, out of my head. The thing I couldn't understand, buried. Safe, safe. I hid my feelings from the trees, so they could sleep and stop asking each other: Who was she? Did she know what she felt? Was she lying? Was she lying to herself? That's how it went for me.

Was she broken now? I didn't know how to connect, and then it was too late. I worried over the rainbow that cornered us, frowning, while we waited for the bus.
With nothing else to do and everything wrong done, I did what I had to. I bit my tongue and fucked my head against a wall for two days.

if there's something else, it's not here

so goodbye
to people
all people
I should have known

here I've made a *near*
a minute sit
the feet trip
in all the hats adieuing

and you bark
"if there's something else
it's
not here"

inside I've died
and laid
home to rest
placed my tomb bed
against coal

hell
it doesn't fit

so goodbye
if missed
tell
it wasn't
them but i

if that doesn't work
lie

so
got to go
alright

Part Two
O Barcelona place I go to die. The Fight.

What do you do abroad?
- Get lonely, find some old strings, tie them together.

Why do you go?
- To fix what came apart

Near Tapas Victor (Day 1)

Men at the next table, hard men, tough men, floral print muted tees cutting at bloom of bicep. One has tattooed knuckles he doesn't seem to regret.

In the falter of proud English, they order Spanish food, wide-eyed dance of creatures attempting to avoid a shock while climbing a fence. Four coffees, loose jokes.

I think they will burn in the sun, but they hold. I think they will wilt, not having control.

Until one says "alright chaps" meaning "we can go". And that is just that. I sit alone and the sun comes for me now.

I order a double espresso, not soft. Un café con leche y bikini, not uncomfortable.
I think and think and think.

Stubbornness' become pink as that morning's dawn.

Outside Hotel Illort (Day 1)

In the square outside El Triangle, there are single-spaced benches. The old men sit to look at people passing. The only young people are women staring at their phones.

I write, resist nature for it is more natural now than staring to pull out the comfort of the black screen. It ties us to our people the same reason the old men watch theirs, so as not to fear.

Fashion and accents billow, pass us, billow away. No path nor function, sight and sound.

I have been awake on and off for twenty four hours for seven days. The heat dizzies.

At this point, I'm becoming afraid. At this point, I could quite easily fall.

TEN

Los Ramblas (Day 1)

You will make your way down to the beach to see the sea at night.

Yes. You will feed the bread you kept for breakfast to any birds you find there, and send them. To home, to the hostel, to the Americas, to your kin, your lost hearts, you're past. That should take a *good* hour.

You will ignore the stands with little ornamental fans, you will ignore the old men, still sitting after hours. You will ignore the young tanned men throwing spinning lit up toys into the potential air for children and drunks; though appreciate the neat way each one seems mythic, a wisp leading you ahead. Ahead:

Ignore the ladies selling flowers, you will not bring flowers to the sea, you are not mourning. Ignore the smell of the Mediterranean here on land. It is just the seafood restaurants urging you to stop.

You will accept the trepidation doing something for yourself brings. You will not accept that all strangers bear you ill will.

Follow the wisps to the beach to see the sea at night to feed the birds. You will walk centre and in the light of Los Ramblas, and listen to them come and them go; the words to feed the birds along with the bread.

This is how memory is remade.

NINE

The Lake/Fountain Lady Looks At Me (Day 3)

The bubble-blower gave out to me for his photograph taken unsold. I have no money for street vendors so I sit at a distance and watch the children with no idea of consequence go catching, catching

Surely this is the true meaning of making new life –

the bubbles are giant deep sea alien fish who last only a minute and then –

go. I don't like to know or think about bursting, I feel like there is a physics we don't know that shifts things from our vision and they become part of the air and we swallow them in, we breathe them and they are not burst, just something no longer understood.

There is no one to share this moment with; is this what death is? The air smells of bread and washing detergent. Pigeons gather ear to ear to hear about how to make life, ignore the art.

rebecca leanne claire gimblett

EIGHT

Old Town (Day 3)

Do people think this is old- or town-like? When I come out I go back in again, getting back on the slow ride, I feel like I don't need to think here, or all I do is think here, express interest in the goods until the price. I hear in a French accent "it's a maze" and wonder if it's my ancestors telling me secrets from beyond the grave. I like to see but not touch.

One dark alley I went through hurt me with its fear but I needed it, all around walls with glass encrusted windows, hissing at me, the back kitchen of some fancy restaurants on los ramblas, I needed it, to see the difference between old and new, it's sunlight, which will never reach these flagstones, no matter what time of day.

SEVEN

The tree planter (Day 1)

A voice from everywhere I've come from, the tallest man is short. He looks archaic, even sleazy but he says he plants trees in British Colombia, Alberta, he says he makes money to live by saving the planet, he says he's not a lifer but he'll be there the next five years.

He steals trees, he says, after the season is over, three hundred or so to plant where he wants, in his favourite places, Vancouver Island, back home.

He was in a mental asylum, he says,

you wouldn't think to look at me but the first year after my first season I couldn't readjust I still don't have a phone or ambition just trees sometimes anxiety and a positive demeanour.

He says that he was holding onto an incorrect belief.

What else is there?

I would plant him nowhere, wish him blessing as a blowaway seed.

Nevermind (Day 4)

Even trying to separate we connect anyway.

In the ladies bathroom, a young girl asked me who was singing and we talked about bands that no longer bring out music. She was cute, a virgin mary herself but not as proud or vain as the one painted on the door in graffiti colours meaning "women". Is that what we are?

Outside where the scene disappeared, cervezas and bums, sold on the street and South, little-boy-desperate for a rambling buddy, wanted to go on that adventure and I wanted to see what would have gone with us

> but what if the moon is gone for me, what if, I needed a second, need then a minute, oh well whatever

SIX

Beratcho (Day 4)

The sand hurt my feet but I ran anyway. It was a relief to cross another sea off my list. You talked about feral things, tropic cascades. I told you we should all die out.

Up against a dock frame, we man-and-woman-handled. I thought about gruelling things, how wonderful a good pay-off. Don't wonder about this, it isn't negative. Not mineral or vegetable either. The sand hurt my feet but I ran anyway.

Hipstel (Day 2)

Here I fill the toilets with blood, I still think its penance for bad behaviour and remain silent and don't think of cancers or internal wiring.

I would rather be dead than ashamed (we hate what we can't control).

I scold myself intermittently.

That said, it's better here, I'm not running towards the next five-minute-escape.

Many times a day, away is appreciated. The end feels itself enter the room, flexes its hands, looks for gloves.

Wait/Train (Day 3)

You must turn those seconds, their unhelpful crap, into magic, someone said. All seconds are real, if you can manage to make them so.

I go somewhere interesting, even this is still the question of "can I".

(If I can, this is it: nurture) With every wait, I lean to bring myself into the space.

Back in the real world, I have close friends.

I can see what it'd be like to be really away, I can see how hard I'd have to work if I came back – they won't take losing me twice! T-

-his time to trees. Howth gorse. Jungle fever. We've been through most green.

And time; waiting is root eclectic, bark sacred, the step away from reality at the first delay of a minute.

(But) when it came to go or wait, I always loved nature more.

the Common room (day 7)

Life is just part-time experiences of fulltime chosen or unchosen events.

Here, not there. Here the coffee was lightly foamed on the top so the biscuit gingerly made a desert of it, and I felt rich.

That music I wouldn't have chosen suits the room, here could be a living room with just one-two-many extra tables. Here the sizzle of hot food being melted in a pan that will keep a life or two at bay, pacing. My own feet strangle themselves in pace for another day.

Here I can feel not too hot or too cold and not too alone or too wasted. To this world, I am a part. The person in the corner reading books curling her right hand to her cup though a plate has been provided. People will see the phone, the music, the key with the screwdriver, a person at a table meant for three. They will remember me as a runaway. Plus daffodils in the window. Life goes on.

5 Espressos (Day 3)

tell me, what's his name

Remove yourself from the chaotic spin of others, where possible, don't bet on fights you won't survive, won't win and aren't needed in. People pry, stick to your depths like barnacles on old ships, this isn't bad but if you choose limpets, choose well. Some hang on the wards you give, some demand your arms and legs, a few tear your heart from you, one will claim your middle part.

tell me, are you still

You better know it, before it's gone. It might be years til you get it back and then? Hearts look better in the mirror. Minds can't be given away for nothing. Souls are different kinds of fish; once caught, free to take.

And I gave my wards so easily, they were beautiful, starry borders and dark cliffscapes. It wasn't nothing. It wasn't something.

are you just running away?

At the Bunker (Day 9)

If I had an enemy here, but I don't.

Call of the void, null and avoided, so I don't.

Just… I try. Celebrate all the two sides, opposite Mont Juic. And I was thinking of nowhere else, but also not of here.

I was thinking if they pushed me over into the bush below. I wouldn't mind the tense of it, the forever fall.

I'd be singing my father's football songs and laughing, remember that time…

I would thank my enemy, for sending me home. Put their coins in my whitewashed Roman eyes myself.

rebecca leanne claire gimblett

NOT REAL (Day 8)

I don't have to be seen with the pens and papers, but they come with me anyway. An anchor of sorts, or shroud, or magician's cape.

My nails are many times longer than when I started, it seems they thrive on cheap wine, now that I've passed on moving to the next step. The little white flecks in them are smaller too. Maybe I can survive.

My body is thinning, toning up except in the middle where I swell each night. It is only my mind I appear to be destroying with that unclear fog.

I run in circles telling myself That's Not Real, that's not real, note facts and put the rest in the trunk for some later which paces by the window, looking out, the coffee cold.

Hauntings at the Hour of Noon

FIVE

rebecca leanne claire gimblett

La Sagrada Familia (Day 8)

A park is peace across the way, built for looking, safe.

I am trying to reform, counting, taking stock of limbs. I may have switched important things inside for the others, busy busy.

I am Ganesh of many hands, St. Brigid's Cloak. I am algae farms holding hands across the ocean. Wider wider, juggle juggle.

Friends are sweet perfume on sweet perfume – dependence. I cannot go where you are going, it would be a breach of what and who and why.

I came to the church to remove this peach from me, finally seek God. Here I am, at His house, nothing but incensed.

Hauntings at the Hour of Noon

FOUR

rebecca leanne claire gimblett

The tree planter (Day 5)

It's common courtesy. I have allowed the symptoms to form. I have found that it's easier to accept the inevitable, allow for it, side-track it, outsmart it.

Rather than attacking or attracting it directly.

This time I think it will work.

If the dilemma accelerates, I allow me to be the sacrifice. Fall to knees and hope it's temporary. A sink pulling me in.

His hair is soft as butter.

Friends would all laugh and say of course of course of course.
Some may even like him, it doesn't matter. I find comfort that he's there and they aren't.

I bought a bottle of wine we will share later. I'll make him play his songs for new guests and joke about him stealing me away to the forest.

Joke.

by The cathedral, before (day 9)

Under sagrada familia, small white birds glitter in the trees, they have no interest in climbing any towers even with no need to pay in. They talk from tree to tree, bitch about the wind. I have settled in to not knowing, I'm more at peace than them?

I'm beginning to see what I've been missing, my little birds. My bones are dissolving here, knitting new inscriptions. I am becoming engraved, it doesn't hurt as much as you would think, to breathe, it doesn't break as much to be loved and abandoned though I am not loved, so how abandoned?

Where once this would have killed, birds, it doesn't. Things that seemed important now are not.

rebecca leanne claire gimblett

THREE

Hauntings at the Hour of Noon

TWO

rebecca leanne claire gimblett

By the bedroom balcony window, undecided (day 6)

I work the elongated morning as hard as the building troops, next
door, or downstairs, or in the walls.
I think a city convincingly places hammering noises to lull its people
into feeling things.
Anger. Calm. A sense of moving forwardness.
I am the fate and times girl I try not to be.
Trying. I feel that's key.

I am pressing the planting year between pages,
November to April, UK, if you can get it,
not get but catch
its elusiveness off the net.
January, prepare; Canada blooms in May.
You remember may. Followed by be.
Followed by loss.
I eat less. I walk more.

I sit under cherry blossoms to get to know them,
if they ignore me, their masters might.
Typical, us slaves. Typical, our thoughts.

The porch, undecided (Day 6)

It is sunny out here but you are alone, you will not be cow-driven to be social but you do not want to miss the fun. You feel another sleep coming on. Another sleep. You feel hungry, lady, for yourself. Your body is unhibernating but aware you might be finally listening, is demanding human rest. I want to be able to say no to everything, not just miss out on being asked.

deconstructing To The basics (Day 1)

1. Familia

Lovers are not always couples. Old Spanish women hold onto each other dressed in winter coats, denying the new sun in its minute victory, their small ancient amore follows them down the street, removing lust from the equation like their hands from pockets, so to steady.

2. Family

Those whom we don't choose and who we are free to hate as we see fit, but taught to do so quietly so they don't see. But not us, not me.

Away from home, I am closer to finding, and I find it: I am grief. This is grieving.

3.   Familiar

Denial is gum on the wheel of acceptance. We start off needing, then forget. Until the shaky knees, those damned beats in the heart. There is only a small hope; being in company helps remove it for a moment. A planted flower on a mass grave.

ONE

The tree planter (Day 7)

Smacking fucked lips on a glass of two euro wine, I ache
to use them to lick your calves. Stretching yawned arms,
I want to try on your jeans. How close love is to dreaming.

Please touch my hair, seek its undercurrents
like a gypsy reading tarot. Invite me out
for a nightsmoke. A sip of your warming beer.

I would take each finger to bed,
ask you
to grow a beard.

I would make my drastic body
reaching out
mean careless movements
in a soft machine.

How close love is to dreaming.

ZERO

rebecca leanne claire gimblett

Tree Planter (Day 10)

Here I sit, doll-like.
I cannot try your socks on.
Smell your nostrils. Lick your tongue.
I cannot bury your dead pets.
I cannot place your bets or switch phone calls
between your god and mine.

How close love is to dreaming.
A stony hopeless thing.
Reducing always to always,
wishing for the wishing
impossible any way anyway.
so many so many so so manys…
screaming tearing shaking
I am the same the same the same.

.

Hauntings at the Hour of Noon

rebecca leanne claire gimblett

before it fades, copy and paste this, change where necessary, press send

Hello < >

~~hope the~~ ————————— ~~was~~ ███████████. I want to write while the sentiment remains strong and isn't deadened. Too much time or fear. There have been few figures that appear as if stones cast into my life and act as serious <catalysts/muses/waves of ethereal golddust sent by a god I didn't realise I believed in/detriments> just when █ ███████. And that's what you were, I think, in lots of ways. You are a <beautiful magic fucked> person, <rare, and super unaware of it>. Keep doing what you're doing because it seems to be/is working (/s), I am so grateful to have seen that(/s). ~~If you ever need a place to stay in~~ ————————— ~~, you got it. If you need someone to jump ship to the~~ ————————— ~~to set up a <surf and book shop>, you got it. Do come visit at some point, and~~

~~stay in touch~~ think of me

if and when it tickles your fancy

<*Love*>

Part Three
W.A.S.T;E.land

what do you do if gone, you can't come back?
- figure out how to unknot the bows

(How to) approachingSkyscrapers

1.   The Bowerbird

is the only animal
"I must pick this" to make art in the wild
carves its nest in assorted "Oh I must have this"
frivolities, jotsam, flotsam, "will she – "
the nest itself is only plain, made out of "will someone-"
curved branches, ground bared "anyone"…
"I must…" five were found to have made… "not enough"

2. decorate a structure

The satin bowerbird belts out basic music.

nest art wood jewel (dual)(duel), ring/rang, wrung

maypole bowers; sticks around a sapling
        hut like roof
avenule bower
        two walls/vertically placed sticks

shells leaves flowers feathers stones berries plastic items coins nails
rifle shells pieces of glass

colours match the
                    preference of females
tasting the pain the males have daubed on the walls

play to the transfer effect: cute boys, less elaborate
                        dullcoated swabs, build palaces

react to the discomfort of females, reduce intensity of a

                                        potentially

threatening courtship

No bower, those drummed up tooth-billed b-birds, rape

3. **how to express oneself, that it is
    communication that unlocks
    and sure it leads to things,
    opening up always does**

The Bowerbird isn't sinister. Maybe he builds because expression is
the only way to get through a [nine to five]. If you look at the separate
letters of each of these words, they are mostly unique, yet discernible.

He makes do [There are many types of us] taking minutiae
from nothing, parts suaded, up on our ocean
we, the corrugated roofers, dodgy street laptop
merchants, unlock technology, scripting old
parts, scarf-knitters, leftover scraps of childhood
bound, dandled between fingertips we struggle on with,
There is no one job these days, no [nine to five]
there are bitmaps. we have subscribed. outside
the realm of enjoyment or pleasure, old arcane magicks
church and marriage die.

we need these things like stars need eyes
to watch them, make sure they exist [for] a reason.

we, the junkyard celebratists, samplers of inequity, sharers of responses

emotional scientists

broad spectrum antibiotics

4. to share my over optimistic seldom tried or tested thoughts

[you]

       the male satin bowerbird
       evolution has made
       communicate to understand
       here is a blue shellfish
       the same royal of your eye
       here is an old coca cola bottle-cap
       the year our parents were born
       the colour of sunburn, summer child
       little ones of the north, no less than fifteen
       periwinkles, unique, mona's browless eyes

[These are dotted between, there's so much more out there you haven't found to be]

5.   It's the words not the page

"So far this year's been quiet
up by the lake, jake is doing great
unrhyming couplets, unhinging yeats
from innisfree
[original]
and fake names are coming in handy, fake places, streets
I pretend to have rustled, insulted skyscrapers
I suggest, lay at the bottom
of looking up, when they ask me how to approach
in cities, Niamh has tried to bury her head, sonnets coming
out her
sonnets, at this age? Romance is dead!
…or is it, maybe she's onto something there
Diarmuid sure has been keeping an eye out
too clinical, that background in [whispers] science [scratches
head]
keeps a theory book beside the bed
collects information, see the withering glare"
see his abandonment
see his head expand
see his house being built

Choose your own adventure [+2 for good luck]

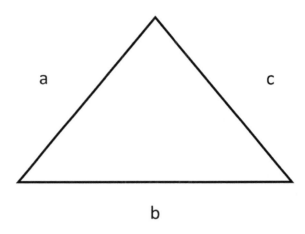

I will add more sides

as true perturbences happen

less to choose from but choose again and again, begin at

   ➔ a   and learn about love
   ➔ b   melancholy
   ➔ c   writing

angled disaster intakes of breath

once or twice a year all ghosts come back

embittered I cannot go on, I sit at their graves and wish for their bones
to heal

underneath, silk worms steal the work of spiders, knitting heart
muscle and shoulder

blades, solitude is building for them, sadness answers none of their
questions but asks

is there art in purpose, love in art, words in love

rebecca leanne claire gimblett

Begin Boat Experiments

a fine wave, containing particles tightly ground as seeds in a coffee pot, sometimes wakes me startled from the slumber that makes up our life, I tell myself

"It was my soul".

picture: small to medium to goliath to god

picture: book hysteria fucking us up

Problem 1: As a lover waded out into a river and burrowed until water clung ball-gowned to her, is it dreadful, to be reminded of anything?

Explanation 1: The dichotomy here is that if it isn't water you walk through, rush into, what do you be? Talk yourself out of the equation, you get:

Instructions:

skip a stone to save her

if you hate water, then…

if you've never loved, then…

if you've never felt alone, then…

if you don't know what a bowerbird is… then

if you want to be a poet… then

⇨   if not, move forward one poem.

Aristotle Categorises Pluto or THINGS THAT MEAN NOTHING

Contd.; Substance. Quantity. Qualification. Relative. Where. When. Being-in-a-position. Having. Doing. Being Affected. [Paschein]

plutoplutopluto
say enough to make nothing
from it; from him?
planets feminine: venus. earth.
planets masculine: mercury (featherfeet). mars (war). Jupiter (zeus).
Saturn (why).
                    Neptune. Uranus.
the O signifies manliness; rename to Pluta?
she is ~~small cute petite~~ scared
first we giveth, then we taketh away. persecution, anyone else?
Jesus. Galileo. Ghandi… Sa… Martin. John.
Joan. We gather first name bases to litmus test the quality of the sting.
Pluta what?
L'abime… but she is a roman girl, pluta in roman? Profundum
Abyssus why not [Persephone] herself
why not Hades, the name of the place itself
No, Pluto.
First we taketh. Then we giveth.
Dwarf King of the underworld.
We are the world.
Her heart under us.

The world gave	positives	which made me give unto the world	positives
divorce	stepparents	escapist, cut and runner	hobbies
emotional abuse	cynicism	fear, lashing out	learning
depression	empathy	ticking time-bomb	inevitability-bred calm
abandonment by love	experience	chaotic, unpredictable, abandoner of love	art
sexual disempower-ment?	potential? the search	quick to anger, upset?	**won't let happen** ~~**again again**~~ **again?**

The migration path of animals versus time

afraid to build new connections and BLAZE NEW TRAILS we exist
upon the world's old motor neurons, we are its thoughts firing, each
birth and death as natural as learning a new phone number, forgetting
someone's birthday, being afraid of anything is the real flick of the
switch

triggers: local climate, availability of food, season of the year, mating
reasons

obligative OR facultative

obligative: must migrate

facultative: choose migration

monarch butterfly, painted lady
never reach migration holy mecca
mate and die on the journey
babies make good fellow travellers
swallows hibernate under water, mudholes, hollow trees (what a small
thing; everything)
wildebeest, salmon, penguins – madness – escape

can art leave the wastelands?
can words?
when does it become real?

rebecca leanne claire gimblett

the art of travelling through a piece of poetry – climate, mates, food
obligation, must [fate]
facultative, choice [free will]
a calling
(what a small thing; everything)
the hour of noon is a migration, day to day

Options:
follow
set down
choose at random, stay or go

stay or go
Lena said there's two ways
to tackle this world
two successful ways

either you fight it
or you smile at it

strapped to a fight or left in a tight glitch
there is no backward pass to life
no way to return to previous moments
no way
no way
wrong

though conquered we will not be subdued

Part Four
THE HOUR OF NOON

"Whoever thou mayest be, beloved stranger, whom I meet here for the first time, avail thyself of this happy hour and of the stillness around us, and above us, and let me tell thee something of the thought which has suddenly risen before me like a star which would fain shed down its rays upon thee and every one, as befits the nature of light. - Fellow man! Your whole life, like a sandglass, will always be reversed and will ever run out again, - a long minute of time will elapse until all those conditions out of which you were evolved return in the wheel of the cosmic process. And then you will find every pain and every pleasure, every friend and every enemy, every hope and every error, every blade of grass and every ray of sunshine once more, and the whole fabric of things which make up your life. This ring in which you are but a grain will glitter afresh forever. And in every one of these cycles of human life there will be one hour where, for the first time one man, and then many, will perceive the mighty thought of the eternal recurrence of all things:- and for mankind this is always the hour of Noon".[1]

---

1 *Friedrich Nietzsche

The Anatomy of Time

As constructed between point A and point B

where seconds are determined in real time (present continuum) and in definite amounts (the trap was entered upon September 2013 OR August 2013 OR two weeks after the rest of the class; the trap escaped in August 06 2014 OR April 2014) where methods and moments will be discussed and defined and eliminated.

Where conceptual time: "She wrote that in one week… in two hours within one week… her whole life lead towards that moment" where words themselves are a construct of time, place, origin and choice.

Where the time of the poem itself comes into play; is there a construct of time within the poem, does it span memory and if not, how long does the reader/poet need to read it, how long should they take to read it and is this one that is/should be taken into account

where time is repeated (how long between poems are read again) and time is distance between poems, where it is also distance between ideas, where one can linger dutifully over the obvious and skip through the flotsam and jetsam – where the need to linger over this and that is ill defined and impossible to determine, we allow a freefall of time, we can gain an average.

where time is the time of day the poem was constructed versus the time of day/year the poem was read

where time is the years of age of the person – all people involved – which also ill-defined but generally can describe a general mentality

time travel. is it possible?

where time travel = $\dfrac{\text{past experience x time (X)}}{\text{current existence}}$

where X is the movement back to a certain time, idea, moment with the knowledge of past experience of that moment and the ability to change – with indulgence – the experience.

If everything is documented, so all seconds are accounted for, it is possible to go back, as technology proceeds. You cannot change. it is impossible. You *can* experience again.

where time is changeable, it is unstable. where stable, it will always be there.

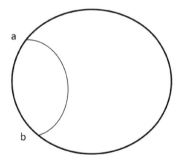

Two points, connected. Time is made up of infinite a's to b's, each one occupying its own space in the circle

-is there infinite?

- is time finite? This is dependent on time repeating itself or ending at some point. The order of connection;

> if we write about *everything*, we can travel there; moment to moment.

Gates and doorways, halls and hallways, things opening, fitting spaces, crawl spaces, underneath, below, downstairs, between, windowsills , fireplaces. Sometimes eternity is legend, an imprint.

If we write about everything, that is the gate to travel there.

rebecca leanne claire gimblett

Part Five
Hauntings. The Infinity Knot.
What happened. Will happen.

What if you can't change anything?
- Even that is learning something.

I am writing this at 7 o clock in the morning and I am trying to tell you goodbye. My head swims with distaste that you still exist in this world that I also exist in. The breath I save for long extinguished candles wasted on trying to speak with you, I am writing you this note so that you might understand something about me.

The stare of Californian sun on the corroded lines of my heart has caused a burn.

Looking through the window at you sitting out in your garden unable to even be in the same room as me is causing drowsiness and other sub-factors associated with heavy medication. They told me that you were not one of the good ones, they told me these after many months of me telling it to them. When I explained about whom my current boy was, the first thing I had to say was our story, and the second thing I had to say was 'Yes, it's very romantic but really, he is not a very good guy'. Back before this entrapment here in your house in LA, I suffered no disillusions.

Now I try to think that I am here on holiday. I try to forget you as feet pad across the floor in your sister's room at 6am. I am caught in a constant time zone of ache. I cannot tell the difference between this and the pain of a friend dying.

Each word I try to think of to explain seems more inadequate than the last. How do I explain to you about a building being demolished, a leaf shattering under a foot? When I took the flight here, I told them all that I was going to my ruin, jokingly not joking, and they asked me not to go.

They couldn't understand what made me run to you, and I will never admit how much those flights cost. They cost five hundred euro. I borrowed it off my parents who cannot afford it. I told everyone that it was something that I needed to do; it was something that had to run its course.

In my own head, I assumed it would just be like before, that we would get back to who we were and something would happen. When I think about the money and how I was paying for my own destruction, I weaken my resolve to end things all over again. I want to make it work with you. I have to. I *have* to miss your kind words. I *have* to try and email you another message asking what changed, why I am here and you are not. Why you cannot stand to be in the same room as me, that it is ok that you miss your ex-girlfriend, show me how much you miss her…

And then I remember the fucking. The three times you fucked me, I wanted it so badly. That's why I had come, to be fucked. It's all we ever had between us, wasn't it? You never lied to me about that. You picked me up at the airport and your confusing hesitation before planting a kiss on my lips and trying your tongue in my mouth floored me more than the coldness of the kiss. The cold leather of the kiss. Your mouth was circular and hard like a buzz-saw that hadn't been turned on yet. I could feel the spikes of it starting to grow in my mouth, ripping out the gums in my cheeks and stealing my tongue organ from me.

The drive from the airport took too long. We stopped for a burger in your favourite diner and I tried to make small talk. I hated myself for that, hate small talk. I should have done better, made you normal by sparking some interesting debate. I could see the distance rowing between our eyes whenever I made a comment and panicked, so that when you mentioned that you had forgotten how cute my accent was, I perked up like a little lapdog and leant all velocity into that.

The first time you fucked me was on your sister's bed, I didn't even make the cut to yours and hadn't yet seen your room. Though I had tried my best to remove every last hint of personality from my body the last month in the lead-up, you didn't notice. I had forgotten that this was LA and all the women had marble who-am-I bodies honed by stress and starvation and exercise. I had forgotten that this whole city was a snowglobe where all the crazy perceptions that women create in their heads are in full swirl. The rest of the world look at it and steal ideas from what they see but this is where it starts.

You took me hard and you took me rough. You once had been a considerate lover but somehow you mixed up my inclination towards a more carnal tete et tete with the thought that I like to be used and abused. There are so many things you don't understand about me.

I did not enjoy the sex but I enjoyed the closeness. I thought that it was the beginning of something turning around. I expected a lighter version of you post-coital to relax and open up about what was going on with you. I knew that you were depressed and on medication for panic attacks. You had told me weeks previously, and I thought it had bonded us, that sharing that information with me made me special but here I was in LA trying to help you, trying to save you, and you weren't talking, you were fucking me.

I tried the "desperate female" art of cuddling after, and you running out of the room after one minute of me trying to enforce closeness shook me.

The second time you fucked me was on the couch in the back sun room. It was the second morning when I came and tried to sit quietly in the same room as you and hold my breath and not count the seconds until I knew you would move into a different area. I couldn't understand what was going on and why there was a canyon between us but I was still too afraid of the true answer to ask. Your laptop was open and you finished talking to whoever was online and made a grab for my body. I had told you that I was on the pill for the three weeks I was here and so we didn't use condoms. This time was a little better. I was so tense from the two days of silence and confusion that I needed the roughness of your body to release me.

After climax, you walked off again but this time I didn't expect anything. I assumed that this was the way it would be and that maybe after a few days, it would get better. I emailed my friends and told them that the atmosphere was full of boulders here, but that it was ok. I told them that it would probably take a few days to get better. I told them that the weather was glorious and that I was enjoying the break from child-minding.

The third time you fucked me was on the kitchen floor. It was the next day and we had been to see one of your friends that evening before because they had a pool that you assumed I'd want to use. I was too conscious of my body in front of a stranger to undress. She seemed intelligent and you had told me in the car on the way over that if she was a little prettier you'd marry her in a heartbeat. You both mostly talked about people I didn't know and I tried to make a list of things I could say to impress her and to impress you if the opportunity arose that I could say them. I didn't swim, but I didn't do too badly. I was introduced to her as a friend and nothing more was said about how we knew each other.

She asked about your ex in Berlin and you said you missed her but that she was there and you were here. I shattered into a thousand pieces. I had seen a music playlist with her name on it on your computer but had assumed that it was something she had created for you and hadn't worried. I knew she had terrible taste in music. You had told me months ago, when you followed up with 'She's not you'.

Hearing that you missed her and it was only distance keeping you apart brought me to a level of realisation that I could no longer ignore. When we got home, you kissed me in the hallway and then stopped. Taking my hand you brought me to the kitchen and laid me on the floor taking off my clothes. On top of me, I could see the look of no feeling in your eyes tinged with panic and began to have an attack myself about what the hell was happening to me, what was I letting happen to me. When you finished, I got up and walked away.

I went to your sister's bed, which was mine for the moment as we didn't share one, and laid down and stopped caring. I tried to make myself very small and breathe slowly to know that I was still alive. This was unlike anything that had come before. My body went into full protection mode and I could no longer keep the mask on my face that had allowed me to pass through the last few days without showing what I was thinking. I laid there wide eyed on the bed and wanted nothing more than for it to be my coffin. When you walked past the open door and saw me, at first you did nothing and passed by. Then you came back and asked if I was ok. I said yes without looking at you and contrary to any other time in my life that I was not fine and told people that I was fine, I did not want your company or questions. I was falling apart and didn't want you around. You took my answer and disappeared again for a while.

I put on some music, a particular heart-wrenching song on repeat might make me cry and feel some relief. But I felt nothing but a sinking feeling, as if my body and mind were removing me as much as possible from the situation because if I was truly to feel the pain of it, it would be too great. I emailed my friends that I had been mistaken, that they had been right and they could tell me they told me so. I told them that I would stay; my penance for bad decisions would be the full brunt of the consequences. I had no more money for flights but I knew that they would pay for them if I asked. I didn't. They offered anyway, I refused. I would take this punishment. I didn't miss the old you, the emails, the intense whirlwind romance we had created. I didn't miss anything yet, that feeling was too distant from the shot-put of pain in my chest.

And then you came back into the room. Stood awkwardly in the door. Explained how it was different that you expected, that you could tell I was trying to fill a place, that you are just out of a relationship that you didn't want to end and you are not ready for the cloying closeness of me. You didn't say those words but you weren't too far off. It was so simple. I had gotten everything wrong, expectations raised by a man who is used to saying 'come visit me' to girls and not having it really happen.

But I could tell too that you were broken. It was what I could never explain to my friends about your attraction, you were me. I knew that. Maybe not just then, lying on your sister's bed, wondering if I had let myself be raped, but I knew that we were each other. You had forgotten, and I know it isn't naïve to assume that. You also might have been looking for something that wasn't like you, I could allow that also, but I also assumed you were wrong in this. That you were just blinded by your own pain and anguish from the mental illness that was currently taking your mind hostage to see that your ex-girlfriend wasn't right for you.

I was desperate. I had a syndrome.

I nodded and you left the room and after a long time feeling sorry for myself, I fell asleep. It was the first time in three days that I slept more than a couple hours. In the morning, I came to find you in your bedroom and shout at you. It took a lot for me to do it; I had never been good at anger or needing retribution.

I was desperate. I had a syndrome.

I shouted at you for ignoring me and moving from room to room so that I felt like I was chasing you around the house. I shouted at you for being so melancholy all the time. I shouted at you for trying to set me up with one of your friends so that I would be out of your hands. I shouted at you for abandoning me at any opportunity. And you smiled a bit because you could see how hard this was for me and then I started to smile and demand to be taken seriously because of the relief of not being shouted at back. I told you I didn't expect to be taken anywhere; I was there for a holiday. I told you that we would not be having sex again and that you were not allowed to have sex with anyone else while I was here.

There were ground rules and it was the first time we laughed about something. You told me that I was being too intense and I told you I would back off if you would stop being weird. You apologised for the way I felt and it was a little victory and I realised that I was still in love with you. Even though I knew it was over, I could feel the heavy bands of confusion being lifted away to let my heart soar up again like a cat you thought you had drowned, but I knew better this time and I pulled away, remembering you were sorry I was in love with you.

We went to the Farmer's market and I resolved to make you love me again, even as we had reached this ground of no return. I tentatively asked you questions about your ex-girlfriend testing out each answer for the level of pain it produced and seeing how far I could go. I would become a rock that jutted out into the sea that would withstand years and years of waves thrashing it, never showing the loss and never collapsing all at once. I would become the person who felt nothing and so could do anything.

I wasn't very good at it. The days started going by more smoothly and I would become happy at any little victories such as compliments you would give me, or time that you spent with me that you weren't on your phone or your computer or places you would take me that you thought I might like to see. There were times when the anxiety got really bad and you'd disappear into your room or away and I didn't know was it to talk to her or was it a panic attack and I couldn't ask. I didn't understand what you were going through and thought that you just suffered from mood swings of suddenly becoming close to me and then suddenly forgetting me. I didn't know until later how close to not coming back from this I was.

There were minute by minutes hopes unhoped, like the trip to the concert where I was sure it would come together. You disappeared for most, when you were there it was uncomfortable. I grabbed your hand at Love Is All because I had to, it was compulsory. The ride back that I later found out you hated, that it was your worst moment, was my favourite thing. I still think about that.

And then your hands started grabbing, children at monkey bars. We became an old tv couple. We played ball in the yard and you told me I had good arms. That you wanted children with good arms. I wasn't very good but I wasn't bad. I slipped in leaves and at times tried to think how she would act and whether it would work.

I met your family and we gathered at a museum. I tried to be aloof as a housefly circling a raw steak. Charming as an Irishman. Your sister told me she liked me and it meant it was over. I still refused to believe it.

Time started becoming smaller, loose, I was nearly about to leave before you told me you didn't want me to go. We had become each other's back ache and melted into each with hands built for knots. But never too far. Never far enough. I still thought I wasn't deeply corrupted in a place I hadn't yet thought to look.

On the last morning, I am brave and peel myself into your bed. Your bed, you asleep. Woke you up, an unhappy face but left myself there anyway. We held. We might have done more, you started to make moves but I stopped it, thinking it was a victory. Thinking this was power. But sex is now rage-hate. It is too late.

Back in Canada, I sit open like a safe broken into.

I scurry about and look at the things left behind. Try to remember how I was pieced together from them. They are sharp and they are round.

For weeks I exist badly. Something needs to happen. I want a 'why', and not answered from you. I want a me-why. I need to plan out my life from a to b and time travel to the bits that made me this. So I can come back to this. So I can make light of this next bit.

REDACTED: Diary of The break: Looking in at the world instead of putting it out

6.47pm
How simple it all is how stupid   to be bouncing all over the
place.   It is 6 minutes from when I started timing
THE BREAK.   Do not take push anymore   It's
making you crazy.   Ask him if he gets or has ever heard
of anyone going crazy   ask him why it suits some people
and it doesn't suit others.   get help for your downs
ask him if you should feel embarrassed about   the soul?

it is **6.49** since all the above   does anyone else feel this way?
The time watching is ridiculous, time is so long and so slow
didn't he leave me alone
all I want is for him to be gone   maybe tell him I love him,
make me desperate   make him run

if I go home I'll be free of him
If I go to New York I'll be free of him
If I go away I'll be free of him.....

WHY CANT WE HANDLE RELATIONSIPS   ARE NOT
HEALTHY THOUGHTS
< TELL SOMEONE GET HELP >

6.52pm
why do people do this, it's not fun   I don't want to be the crazy
one
who flew off home to get   on pills or in some hospital bed
(I just thought that rhymed).   How can I be normal again

I have to forget Have to forget   HAVE TO FORGET
STAMP OUT

18.58 twenty minutes from the time and I'm cold and terrified because I don't know if it's because I left the doors open, with the music turned off so they wouldn't hear me wouldn't know that I'm down here, afraid to lie in bed because I need the time beside me and I think they'll come and find me. So cold, maybe they turned off our heating because I'm here and they hate it and I'm rocking back and forth and I'm rocking back and forth. THIS WAS THE WORST DECISION EVER < DONT BE ON YOUR OWN < YOU SILLY IDIOT < IT'S SOMETHING < WHICH YOU DON'T UNDERSTAND > STOP STOP STOP STOP STOP STOP PUSHING> STOP TAKING >

19.02

thinking of what he would say to the above   He told you
already, that's how
it makes people feel, when they are not good   your brain
repressing information
so you can ask him again later my god
you are so sad
how do people bear it
elaine how do you bear it
every day so well

I'm pretty sure earlier I didn't care.   Like coming home
like, like you kind of do
have to move on, you can't just keep   loving the same person all
your life,
he doesn't love you, that's it, move on, he doesn't love you,

it's simple its clear cut

19.05 can once again reassess the situation who cares its fine get music in your ears

19.06.5/7   too paranoid to function shaking knees weak, can't light candles cos he's afraid he will burn down the house grit teeth wondering how to get this message out MULTIPLE personalities Seek Help

19.09 SEE TITLE
19.11 last stop. going to go to bed. hope I survive the night,

19.12
but I'm thinking that this could be your future novel   you   are writing it all down,
so maybe it's just genius part   that this all has been.   I feel like I am the multiple personality, and I tumult   through all of all the seconds of the day.

Choosing one to function for me one day or next,   depending on the one I need. Here comes Paranoid   with the knocks up in the ceiling and they are coming down the stairs and coming to get me they are coming   to get me please help please help oh god oh god   it is 19.16 right now. 36 minutes from start to finish. maybe I just won't hear them, where am I this time

OMG IM ALONE IM SO FUCKING ALONE
PLEASE HELP ME PLEASE HELP ME
ALL THE LIFELINES COME TO HELP ME
THIS IS SERIOUS TAKE THIS SERIOUSLY
Hands shaking. It is **19.18** oh god
I just want to be happy I just want to be happy,
don't let anyone see me as unhappy

rebecca leanne claire gimblett

They are laughing upstairs in the house at me,
I don't even know what date or time it is. It is **19.18** it's fine
right it's fine. I was happy for a large portion of my life
right, what does it mean that I am writing all this writing right now,
what if I read it later and I

more water **19.23** shivering cold terrified **19.24**
I'm doing everything at once. Kill yourself.
You don't have anything to figure out right now

19.26 I can't handle it I hear them on the stairs
and think they are laughing at me, I just want to be comforted,
do I have no theory of mind.
YOU NEED TO SHOW THIS TO A DOCTOR
BUT THATS WHAT EVERYONE NEEDS TO DO (the clue
is it is all coming back to academia, you know that right.
Multiple personalities, they are tumulting for everyone
and this slows them all the way down
so that the weak ones feel it more
than the strong ones and does) everybody feel this way **19.28** cold,
need water

ask him what is happening to you, take him seriously.
No, give him up, he is not worth seriousness,
just stop caring about it (a chaos russian doll)

19.31, time is moving faster again   so this is how it works
this is the scientist, and she is trying to save you.
You have a scientist inside you who wants to save you.
A creative genius/novelist/paranoid to create the beautiful words
head twitch to right

novelist and scientist
are linked as well which leads to
HAPPY WOW SUPER CHIN GRIN TO JAW
REALLY HURT LIKE A BACKWARDS PAIN
(i.e. not at all)
tired sleep

19.33
going to get music
he was crazy about you now he's just using you,
no he loves you he loves you he just doesn't realise
it yet I swear this is what James Joyce did.
envisioned all his different personalities at once
and then he wrote it all down, and it was Ulysses.
maybe he faffed about a bit and aimed the story
in that way but maybe he could be the same
personality as you so you could be as successful
as him if you only had the guts

(and you do, was the point of the last one,
you went Happy, Sad, Novelist,
this guy has a calm voice and he is beautiful
and calm like a sheriff) am i drunk?

19.36, time is slowing down again. so tired trapped within an icicle-
body. I can't contain
19.37
T.S.Eliot, the paper writes, is also of this mind.
He saw his personalities
(oh god I need help so tired sleepy calm)

19.38, are we working in milliseconds now.
Oh yea so TS ELIOT and he put them into Prufock.

i just want to sleep
will elaine be mad.

YOUR PERSONALITIES ARE INFECTING YOUR DECISION
IT IS WHY YOU CAN'T IMPEDE THEM
THEY ARE TRYING TO ALL GO DIFFERENT PLACES

San Francisco, New York, Home cos nothing matters, it's never going
to help
go wherever the fuck you want to go because you are fucking fucking
broken
and you will never be fixed. You will never never be happy and you
have to go home and seek help.
Look if you had some sort of plan it would have worked by now, or if
not, the fact that you are still thinking these things is a bad sign.

rationale, what does this mean
going to bed **19.43**
Tell Elaine that she's right whatever Elaine thinks she is right.
Tell people that you are just about holding on,
pull it all on the line for West. You have a broken heart
and you can't take it anymore Go home to your family,
go home home home. Is this how everybody feels,
is this rational. TELL ELAINE, NEVER AGAIN. Never let her do it
again.

go, seek help at peace with this decision **19.46**
(some things shouldn't be written, shouldn't be read.)

114

Part Six
AMOR FATI. Coming Home.

"is this it?"

"dream, love, suffer; sleep it off!"

1.

as a lover I waded out into the river, borrowed the water until ballgowned. Dreadful,
to be reminded of anything civil, polite, decent, I waded deeper still.
At times my eyes stung, letting in stray drifts as doorsteps do snow.
I circumference the ocean as this creature, shallow breathing air and only stopping
to blink out my eyes.
As a lover, sting meant nothing,
it was cold but not always unpleasantly so.
It reminded me of floating, this terse walk. Except for the willed and unwilled rocks, seaweed strands, stray crabs which always tripped or pulled my weight to their level,
I would fall.

2.

I fell. I had always fallen. I will fall again.

What happened underneath?

3.

I rose, a seafire rushing
over land, coast mama, beach maiden
feast on my weather curses, paint my shrieks
sketch and shade the sky the colour of the light inner circle of my eye
the circle that turns eternally around the abyss

in the small thin vistas
I bathe
the way a skipping stone breathes sliver slips from both worlds
wet and dry, in its final foray

make me not know love but know how to live in two worlds at once
I would have two bodies of water in me
to die in baptism, cry life as I drown

from a gravel birth to a gravel death
bed, let my geodes encompass some part of greatness
difference, finality.
everything, even change, grows small if without end.

The brushwave has come, the curio storm and so what?
Exquisite gulls yak behind my procession
feet clacking the pavement behind a hearse.
below crabs drumroll, the shark moan, my chrysalis body

I steal more words from both worlds
fly and fall between them; apexing, bound
only by nomenclature.

What Happened Underneath

when it was ok that I didn't have a great job but I had a job and it allowed me to write in stolen seconds, make spare parts of the day

when it was ok that the job became bigger until it was a whale mouth with gold in the fillings that I used to buy bread, bartered with salty chunks of my heart

when the words dried slowly in the mud and blood shapes, I had poured them on paper

when the words dried weird and I couldn't see the difference between today and tomorrow, the night-dark of a fishes mouth and the glitter-star teeth

are those the only constellations I'm allowed know

when *where's my dawn?* as torch light sputtered, lit sparely from the pages littering the tongue, also used as bedding. when good and bad couldn't be decided against, for, because, what did that matter

underneath, where molar chatter isn't applause and deep tummy rumbles aren't stamping feet

when I let go of the book, pulled from between cavities, behind tonsil, to cover my empty hands to my mouth to keep quiet

when the sleeping giant was fully asleep

rebecca leanne claire gimblett

then I climbed with knee and nail but eye-blind in one direction, towards the first smell that didn't taste of decay, sting like shit

then I pried those lonely hungry stalagtites from stalagmites, I still kept my eyes closed

it was too soon to consider a life outside an old oath, above my own folly, beneath the want of a martyr's life

then I felt the great slop, the wet of the world on me and I couldn't breathe

when it was a new thing I had discovered, swimming, and I could hear other swimmer's feet mashing the dark between them, going every which way, gathering speed, and seeking

then I took stock, counted only what I had, something that wouldn't have to be put on a page

I reached the surface, tasted meniscus, unchanged, up here work is still work

then I decided not to settle for surface. Pages float up, after me, dried by whales' cries.

Proud Ocean Ox, I am not a sea-baby

and I sought land, and seeking is just writing

and purer, I gained seven years, a reprieve from definite failure

day became madness, I set my time in storylines

and that whale could have spit me out or let me drown but dried me off and dried me out

I saw the power of debt, I was not worried, I had a way

red and white, a lighthouse glinted as some reflection from a glass cloud, acid bright

and I cracked myself open for the first thing that fell out of the earth, a stepping stone, grey, round

when I left, let the first world end, it didn't matter

old book gone, it didn't matter

white moon, chalk smile, still my father and brother

gathered things to me, meant to awaken

a solar wind sister felt things, as I did, sought them, even bilious, to show, thought in action

action in thought, and I felt leaves scatter and I looked above

then the only thing that mattered, was

rebecca leanne claire gimblett

Manifesto
The hope of travel is that we'll stay different,
that it comes with us and not the other way around.
I will take up guitar.
I will not be afraid of bikes anymore.
I will plant trees across the world.
I will no longer care that my lovers are gone or have other lovers.
I will no longer take it upon myself to hate anything.
I will love love love and that will change me,
keep me moved, my first and last thoughts;
come and go.

Part Seven
Living. Existence.

What do you do when you've done everything?
-        Do it again. Do better.

Where Can One Languish As To Be Eternal And Forgotten;
Hold And Neglect One's Own In The Dirt And Slosh Of Time
As A Kissed Coin Sits On The Floor Of Some Wishing Fountain
Crucial To None But Special Perhaps Just To One

In This Dark Limbo Can The First And Final Self-Bloom
Spread, Languorous, Buoyed On By Some Anchored Float
Where Existence Can Be Created And Abandoned
– The Coinflicker Of A Moment –
Brief Unapologetic Life Can Be The Good Death Earned

Integrity

There is shame in thinking incorrectly   "The bastards are in there
living
and not remembering us."

Thinking that someone is wrong   when something is wrong

Or worse   seeing humans   where there are none

We should be: (s)mall iridescent, unafraid of course, doing
reconnaissance, apologising first then storming out

Last words: "I'm not usually this angry…"

No? Then make peace with surface: find
the sun
smug,
brave,
uncaring, pleasuring
itself where it can

be beaver skinned, impossible to make wet

know all your smokes end up   with the ocean floor   all the last
bits
make a splash before we do   let them go   so   when
we're left
we can let go   of these tortures

go home without wondering who is there
leave, trying to be enough   leave, making exceptions
                                    to your rules

          break your finned parts on the honest godly sharpness of
          walls

you must stop trying to put out the fire
you must stop keeping up

you must stop seeing yourself
as anything other than mammal

Confessions in VII Parts

On autumn days I feel of forests even in the city where trees are paper thin or rarecaged animals.

I imagine: whole sidewalks turned inside out, that conkers can be scrambled from underfoot. That oak can acorn and sycamores helicopter, trembling with excitement at the sound of our footsteps nearing, with ease.

I don't fear yellowness or red mess, the sky takes it in of us and feeds, alive, even in this dying season, water turns summer leaf green, ate up on the blowth from trees.

This is the circle that doesn't sleep: I am.

When the day-grey comes, I'm not suddenly afraid. Big buses full up in guzzled children; there is a sense of time and timely growing. I prepare for the white that might come. Increase pouches. Mull wine, blend soups. Stack logs, collect matches…

Madness how houses are familiar magic. We survive the way our parents survived. Spread out. Becoming our surroundings. Anything that doesn't feel natural, gets old fast. I'm going to be around forever.

Those big convoys are us   there   we   are   the   searcher's
paradise   we don't see us as leaves   but   here   we   are
spending time   fall-ing
finding: new news   poems   everywhere   and
regaining childhoodness

All The Wrong Reasons

You perambulate the altar corners I've sworn everything else off of. In niches and notions, you picnic. How has it come to this.

With the blurry end of a red crayon you fixed my brick porch, and all evening all morning, while I sit, you jump at me like kids from cold water. I persist

in finding you in liquid and smoke, I have grown you, up windows and salted you like the lavender graves in the yard. Where comebacks make curses of our prayers, I have woken up beside you.

And you will be the last thing in my life when I die.

Dogs roaming under porches, owls underneath eaves and lost street urchins searching for better tidings might live long last moments but won't ever die alone, if we write them.

You are the fuck in my step. The sex in my stalk. I will die crossing a street, obsessed with digits and ink, I fall asleep undressed next to a warm computer hoping you dream through my fingers and think for yourself on paper asking me to die with you each time.
"Don't leave us alone".

I have not offered you bargains and bribes in exchange for your time, I have held off a leash and not sought you when you hide. We have had our merry chase,
I have made you my murder-husband, and only in this way are we officially tied.

rebecca leanne claire gimblett

Writers, send help, I don't know how to end this. If an end must come, let it be in a whisper to the apocalypse.

Of your own muse and star choosing, keep up business as usual. Stall-worth those appearances, tar and feather us, axe them in competitions, ask for favours, breed the endangered, calibrate your own charts. Even if it is in slow uneasy starts:

don't let our best
die out, without
them, we are
Nothing.

living with it

on autumn nights when you feel you're dying with the growing dark
that all the seconds of the day were killed by your lacklustre that threat
lingering saying you sucked them in
there are no knocks at the door or if there are, they bring people with
long pasts, greater sadnesses than yours and you feel worse. some
kind of void. some kind of black hole, the stone-heart hurts from
black space. when the couch is too big, the sides creeping in red that
you dyed, the other seats greater still, coffee table the wrong size,
drowning.
and no words make sense. the pupils themselves are lying, everyone
doesn't mean to but they do, thinking living better will help. the only
attack is in saying these things to everyone out loud:

YOU'VE GOT TO KILL THE NIGHT BACK.

rebecca leanne claire gimblett

heart

Where did girls learn to draw hearts
on any available surface we could
not anatomical but if the heart
were a piece of fruit
that is more easily
halved.
Anatomically, it is a muddle
cutting into grizzle-flesh would not happen
easily, mark where one vein leads to a cavern
and one to protective but senseless fat
What could we make on paper then, only
the round puberty tops, the singular pointed bottom,
like tears from each eye met at the mouth
simply swallowed.

A real heart can be chunked, like pineapple
Sectors that matter removed along
with the rubbish we don't use,
given away, put to better use. Teary fruit, it isn't.
Along with the lessons of our new crude bodies
becoming, girls should be taught
the real heart, draw it fifty times plan,
and fifty straight on, here is where it goes in,
here out, here it never stays still
cramped and making its one job its life.

Eat that, not fruit, and think of desire.
Not smooth and delicious but meaty, bloody,
satisfying. Eat that.

moonlighting

When I look at my body, I see it
a great Indian pagoda, pleasant in silver
from my husband's coffer or maybe I'm not a mistress;
I can buy and sell men,
they don't know what hour on the clock has just struck when I'm there.

My limbs lie stretched against the bay, holding back
pirate ships bound for the Darien strait, no guerrilla war
can pale vagabond hearts, we remain, are free, can tour.

I shrink and become a walker.
Merchants more angry than god
sell tiny toy Cartagenas or Mexican trinkets
and we laugh
at our simple Spanish, how Babylonian we are.

The velvet grows warm and humid in the jungle.
At night. I take you out and look at you all like a photograph
loved very much.
                    I fear
                                my body cannot take these rhythms.
In real life it racks up and petrifies with the least amount of wind,
whip or other force upon it. I try and hold back the ocean, I crack
and widen and disappear into another continent,

I am learning to take it inside of me allways

rebecca leanne claire gimblett

Left behind
you say I don't know why you were never told that. I don't know why you were never told that. But here I am, in the wonder-sphere, breathing.
Thank you for the teachings; here you aren't.

knowing comfort

The roses are all gift wrap ribbons
stuck on
By the porch where I feed myself so
many minutes
This porch
I've labelled my resting place
Long years will pass
They'll still find my ash here

Though I will leave
I will
I stalk purpose every day
I will witness departure
On my commute, making coffee,
coming back from readings
I will
I'm already planning it
the go
Like a child from sick parents
Or the dog from perfume

I pull mountains to me
From the porch
where runners pass looking forward
And couples argue over shopping bags
And the trash mounts up next door
Our neighbours sweep
the porch
to teach us cleanliness
In all things

rebecca leanne claire gimblett

But this is my grave
I'll do as I please

The roses smell of nothing but reach
Like the smell-grasp of itchy hands
I don't have the heart to cut them back
Even if it makes them stronger
I would let them grow
To block
The one way traffic that pleads
with the street
Not to have people on it

Someone looks after the garden
Fenced black from us
With bushes that are real and real earth
The tree ripe most of the year with red
beady eyes
Doesn't feel real
Isn't allowed overhang
For fear it'll fall

The roses fall
On the porch
Get swept away where they will go
Which is normal
Which is natural
Cleanliness in all things

five burnt wood secrets

i

it goes out
I blame the light
I blame the wind
I blame the piss yellow grass
On the side of the cliff
dry for years, unburnt for decades
Only burnt by the wind
Which I blame, which never stops
And the salt that drifts from the sea
so lonely
And the skin that drifts from our bodies
So lonely
To other bodies
Nothing is itself, even the light
From the sun is tired of his workday
Night to night, no rest, for little pay
And the water, which leaks and stretches
And gets supped by birds mouths
Is not itself, will be burnt
In decades to come, by us.
We cannot sustain a good thing
go mad with the sick order of life
Showers in the morning, baths at night
Food all the time, we starve and go mad
From starving and need always more.
it goes out
And stares horrified at it's becoming
And it's not being itself anymore

rebecca leanne claire gimblett

We cannot abide the change of things
the broken chaos, unbroken, always there
again in the morning
In the air like a drunken lovers oath.
we are supped up, we are not
ourselves.
We are supped and taken out and burnt
Only to yearn
For the whatever creature
That knew nothing
That wanted nothing
That went out
For a reason or no reason
We once were

ii

the spider came from nowhere
King-confident, trident legs
Hoping
And I drew a gasp, not figurative
But little o of horror
My last breath
Will be exact
I imagine
The spider crawled across this book
Before these words crawled
He knew before me, before you knew this
And I didn't want him near me
How dare he
assume we were kindred
or similar enough

To be known, for tough skin to touch
All this nature where I sought escape
And he sought death
From something he thought might be natural
But wasn't
My reaction was to fly away
But I wasn't given any wings
Though the need was great

iii

he wants
escape, escape, escape
not in there: thank you
the bag that never closes
doesn't own you
the pewter move of water
that holds the narcissistic birds afloat
that wrinkles without age
and doesn't care
that sinks fleets and licks children's feet
on no whim but its own
No, escape is only animal-made
delicately shaped and crafted - a spider
having learned will ignore
the grey reflection sheet that promises
a hot love deep beneath
and takes the handsome with the ugly
that grows taller soon as you look
away.
That is not escape, it is a prison
It's inmates all of us that swim

rebecca leanne claire gimblett

some afraid, some sailor
some lovers, some fools
I look down and away (it grows tall)
The spider has jumped from my coat
And dashes into the grass
away, to be fed not by anyone
but its own jail
like anything good
He doesn't know his children
dies for them anyway
they will learn what they will learn
when they will learn it.
The grey beast is dangerous
only to those who care.

iv
After mom, dad had a habit
of not telling us not to do anything
Family need not be family, or visited
rooms tidy or untidy
college taken or left
Good kids, we were
Berated him for being afraid
told ourselves off for him
did good and bad things anyway
Home wasn't far but far enough
the way birds fly across a stretch
of water, nowhere to nowhere, but for some reason
home was always a Sunday evening;
any little thing would make it better.
After mom, I tried to break habits
with new ones; figure out where nowhere

became somewhere; within reason
there is always room for trying
To think differently without giving up
staying awake instead of falling asleep
to the sound and beat of old wings
Looking up and not asking why,
not wondering
If I should

v

This yellow cliff is passed.
I take the chewing gum
I take the spray I think will save me
It says outdoor scent
even though I am outdoors
and it is just dry air in a can
I use it and smell more
Of death
Than before
I should jump into the river, into the
sea, wet is better than death
And the salt will clean
my open wound
There are something's forgiven
And something's not
And some stories are funny
later, for all the trouble involved
but this is not
these secrets should be burned, hidden
for I am too old
to be taking my fuck
with life

rebecca leanne claire gimblett

And too young to be troubling my parents
Who worry because
I do not.

monday secrets

I am going the same way
as my two aunts and one uncle
and my aunt on the other side
my grandmother would call peculiar
to a friend on a Monday
But not me, who she loves so much.
This is about the end.
I don't pack cans or learn Skills
I look to trees and follow birds
listen to them
they know more about this than we do
How one goose arrived early
spooked a man in
Germany and now we'll all
feel it: a blasted winter. I abide
by cold winters after hot summers
They record this and that and plan
to no avail.
My aunts, one uncle, tackled this
the wrong way, went soft, I polish
up, in my next life I'll be a welder
stare at metal the same way I stare
at words now, corrupt. Annomalise them.
in the next world, they'll need words too
and psychology and supervisors
My father says sprinters are
only ten second gods, gods of ten seconds
the next world will be made of hours
the next world will need coffee too,

rebecca leanne claire gimblett

cleaners, salesmen, people who can
take a hit below the belt
that don't require geese to spook
them, but follow the birds around,
around until the squawkers spook and
chase their lover wind to somewhere
they think is safe, where people
(those old gods) will look at them,
soft and finally warm, and only
see doom.

going back, moving forward

i

As it turns out
Out the outward window
Glance those Friday eyes
That seek the danger of a familiar street
Heavy lined in silk trees and carnal lamps
Head back, feet mauling the nightmare pavement
As it lines itself along the cracks
As it goes passed, hood from hair from soul,
legs wary, skin weary, muscles in hands and tiny
blood stream Irish men, as it makes the air around it
yellow and red, as the seconds wait for it to meet
stranger to stranger
As it goes As it went
No different As it turns out
As it happens After all

South stretches, blesses the suit around the sailor, marries the air with his fingers, proud cues unmarred from a break of a day, it is daybreak, old filtered photographs from the 60s keep him in the business, let him away with it. He stretches, fetches today's ordinary prayers, makes light of love, a girl's fetching eyes ask to be deepened, **South** sketches his thumbs to fables with beetroot red crumbs on the unvarnished table, he second guesses the depth of his perception, as the wind blows, as the crow flies, as it turns out, the evening comes, he disappears into a Barcelonan alley, only to alight the other side, the grand canal

rebecca leanne claire gimblett

North writes another masterpiece, six feet deep, the flaws seeping into the ink, noxide green mixed with mescaline, the babies growing up with worrying thoughts, the enemies are closing in, blades are sharpened, luck sought, everything is a grey anger brouhaha, the melancholy shit-sticker salivates over what he thinks. No outside world, no inside jibes, **North** will boogie on a Saturday night, on weekdays he worships the manual with matchstick eyes, cuts out the blinks from sentences, the only eyes are wide.

South meets at the workman's social club, the signed walls painted over, anyone's turf, walls are trees sewn together, **South** stretches, laughter splattering around the room, two easy smiles, friends here at his hips, red ale lips

As it turns out
The paper creates the mâché
The arcane spit out the inside of your mouth,
the yell "I'm done, I'm done",
the low grade rude tin of us
Rouging under any sign of wetness
This marble floor for resting
As it burrows in
As it finds me alive and well
As the burning oaks cry uncle
As the poles try not to be noticed
As the air worries
As the air plots films with the barge man
As the tumescent air corrodes the gulfs
we were supposed to fall in love in
East Coast, I might have bought you rosary beads

East teaches. Good kid. He has good kids. His future stinks of little feet. He hears them in the walls at night, gets up at 5 to run them out, the driveway choked with rabbits, pheasants, oak trees growing slowly to replenish. Good kid. **East** teaches humans to hate happiness, easiness. Strives for fullness, correctness, potential, battles sloths and pomegranates, by 5 he's up, hoarse-struck, on weekends, he fucks. He can't remember small conversation, hates to know the details, doesn't get the right jokes, aches over a piano playing pop, never stops

As it mellows, born in the Bon Secour.
As the hands devour it alive
The red ripe scream allowing drought in through the mouth
As it happens, others happen too, smacked and smiling
As the pure terror of the useless outside in the waiting room
As the modern tiredness of inside jobs
Dispelled by blessed heavy drugs
As the tiny warm ship incubates and further ripens, ferments, yields good fruit
And us kept in the winter
Shovelling snow

East ekes feet inside the club, doesn't dance, doesn't know much of the smoke room, dancing circular itself, the tongue dance, people locking eyes, finding friends, sharing the tips of mouths and grimy palms, cellular data, revoked but they just take more, mushrooms grow in the corners, the barman eyes the tipjar, the mangy flock, the precise clock on the machines, father, son, Holy Spirit, oh he dies for his sins, ours trickle through the ceilinged rooms, down the bow of stairs where East can't keep to himself, it's the weekend, he finds someone

North writes and pounds the metal with his hammer,
brave glorious soul tied down beside a knife,
his pen is cutting, cutting, this life in edits
As the buzz saw wallows thinly in lack of hands
As the colonel marches out the door
As the feet don't belong to children anymore
As the park he signed his youth in
North is a monster at midnight

As the clock-bong of feet on stairs deprives the ghouls of their livelihood
The working class working club, full up
As it went next, the music a blinking lightbulb
Outside the people lining up
And next, next, out in out
Tense feet shifting, hands just beginning to shudder with the weight of night
As three men with much in common never meet
The Fourth sinks from the sky.

West never speaks, sometimes nods,
a translation of drinks and fights, sad eyes,
blank dead inside - first sign - digits calm
now, he's built for reactions
For dodging from dark corners
ocean to Ocean, seas in between,
grass and mountain, **West** is a witch,
he never speaks but sits tendons stricken tight,
choked, spitting up the hour of noon

As it turns back
As the merge of two pin holes in a bent piece of paper meet
As **East** marries pregnant silences with fruitless truths
Truths nonetheless
him and them and you
cannot go back to the workman's social club
not the same way not again
Pale from a Wednesday evening,
pillow marching groggy, or at dawn
As the street ruffles at your worn hood
As the shuffle of emancipated limbs dance no more
The wonder comes of this silk terry cloth street
The stranger you are about to meet
As you turn
As I go

ii

If I ever fill it up
And see that dragonarium breathing fire
I'll let my dragons go
Delete them and all their data
And move to better planes somewhere
scarce my troubles
   (One last cigarette tucked
   One last kiss with just lips
   engines run on angry
   expel all with no fists

When you next see me it'll be done
The knack of what we were
but also the want
And I won't wait
to be missed
Or to miss
Where an hour lasts too long, instead
see, a battlefield with no more risks
the rush passed, days coloured
bodies counted, pray-painted
All the hurry blown away
from the bullet-shaft
Hesitate no more for the decimated
Nod only once to star or moon, noon
has passed so be gone)
And focus on something more real
The things I ignore now in between
the feeding and collecting treasure
the breeding and naming of each scale
I will let them go and nod a thanks
Forgiveness, the final kiss-blow

if there's somewhere else it's not here

so be gone

rebecca leanne claire gimblett

Milton Keynes UK
Ingram Content Group UK Ltd.
UKHW020642101123
432322UK00020B/962

9 781662 940118